W9-BRS-521

ideals® MEMORIES

Memory, hither come,
    And tune your merry notes;
And, while upon the wind
    Your music floats,

I'll pore upon the stream,
    Where sighing lovers dream,
And fish for fancies as they pass
    Within the watery glass.

I'll drink of the clear stream
    And hear the linnet's song;
And there I'll lie and dream
    The day along.

William Blake

ISBN 0-8249-1029-X 350

Publisher, Patricia A. Pingry
Editor/Ideals, Kathleen S. Pohl
Managing Editor, Marybeth Owens
Production Manager, Mark Brunner
Art Director, William Scholz
Photographic Editor, Gerald Koser
Manuscript Editor, Naomi Galbreath
Research Editor, Linda Robinson

IDEALS—Vol. 41, No. 6 August MCMLXXXIV IDEALS (ISSN 0019-137X) is published eight times a year,
February, March, April, June, August, September, November, December
by IDEALS PUBLISHING CORPORATION, 11315 Watertown Plank Road, Milwaukee, Wis. 53226
Second class postage paid at Milwaukee, Wisconsin and additional mailing offices.
Copyright © MCMLXXXIV by IDEALS PUBLISHING CORPORATION.
POSTMASTER: Send address changes to Ideals, Post Office Box 2100, Milwaukee, Wis. 53201
All rights reserved. Title IDEALS registered U.S. Patent Office.
Published simultaneously in Canada.

ONE YEAR SUBSCRIPTION—eight consecutive issues as published—$15.95
TWO YEAR SUBSCRIPTION—sixteen consecutive issues as published—$27.95
SINGLE ISSUE—$3.50
Outside U.S.A., add $4.00 per subscription year for postage and handling

*Front and
back covers
TROLLEY RIDE
Richard Hook*

The Old Covered Bridge

Down in the valley, just over the ridge,
Spanning the river stood an old, covered bridge.
Beneath it the water ran clear, deep and cool,
Where nature had formed a nice swimming pool,
And small, naked boys, feeling bashful and shy,
Would hide 'neath the bridge, when people
   drove by.

'Twas a dark, spooky place to pass through at
   night,
When thoughts turned to ghosts and filled you
   with fright.
But a boy a bit older, with a girl by his side,
Would pause there to spoon on a night buggy
   ride.

A new modern bridge now crosses that stream,
But we'll bet that old timers who pass there oft'
   dream
Of that old, covered bridge that crossed shore
   to shore,
And in memory relive those dear days of yore.

Ernest Jack Sharpe

Photo opposite
COVERED BRIDGE
Freelance Photographers Guild

September

Sweet is the voice that calls
From babbling waterfalls
In meadows where the downy seeds are flying;
And soft the breezes blow,
And eddying come and go,
In faded gardens where the rose is dying.

Among the stubbled corn
The blithe quail pipes at morn,
The merry partridge drums in hidden places,
And glittering insects gleam
Above the reedy stream,
Where busy spiders spin their filmy laces.

At eve, cool shadows fall
Across the garden wall,
And on the clustered grapes to purple turning;
And pearly vapors lie
Along the eastern sky,
Where the broad harvest moon is redly burning.

Ah, soon on field and hill
The winds shall whistle chill,
And patriarch swallows call their flocks together
To fly from frost and snow,
And seek for lands where blow
The fairer blossoms of a balmier weather.

The pollen-dusted bees
Search for the honey lees
That linger in the last flowers of September,
While plaintive mourning doves
Coo sadly to their loves
Of the dead summer they so well remember.

The cricket chirps all day,
"O fairest summer, stay!"
The squirrel eyes askance the chestnuts browning;
The wild fowl fly afar
Above the foamy bar,
And hasten southward ere the skies are frowning.

Now comes a fragrant breeze
Through the dark cedar trees
And round about my temples fondly lingers,
In gentle playfulness,
Like to soft caress
Bestowed in happier days by loving fingers.

Yet, though a sense of grief
Comes with the falling leaf,
And memory makes the summer doubly pleasant,
In all my autumn dreams
A future summer gleams,
Passing the fairest glories of the present!

George Arnold

The Old Porch Swing

I love to sit in the old porch swing
At the close of a busy day
Watching the flames in the western sky
Fade to a rose-touched gray.

I love to watch as the lights go on,
As the evening shadows creep,
And hear the cheeping of drowsy birds
As they settle down to sleep.

I love to watch as the stars come out
Like silver on deepening blue
And to feel the dusty air grow fresh
With the fall of the evening dew.

I love to sit in the old porch swing,
Swaying, for there I find,
In the sweet cool hours of evening's hush,
Contentment of heart and mind.

Virginia Blanck Moore

Photo opposite
PORCH MEMORIES
Camerique

A Song of Early Autumn

When late in summer the streams run yellow,
    Burst the bridges and spread into bays;
When berries are black and peaches are mellow,
    And hills are hidden by rainy haze;

When the goldenrod is golden still,
    But the heart of the sunflower is darker and sadder;
When the corn is in stacks on the slope of the hill,
    And slides o'er the path the striped adder;

When butterflies flutter from clover to thicket,
    Or wave their wings on the drooping leaf;
When the breeze comes shrill with the call of the cricket,
    Grasshopper's rasp, and rustle of sheaf;

When high in the field the fern leaves wrinkle,
    And brown is the grass where the mowers have mown;
When low in the meadow the cow bells tinkle,
    And small brooks crinkle o'er stock and stone;

When heavy and hollow the robin's whistle
    And shadows are deep in the heat of noon;
When the air is white with the down o' the thistle,
    And the sky is red with the harvest moon;

O, then be chary, young Robert and Mary,
    No time let slip, not a moment wait!
        If the fiddle would play it must stop its tuning;
        And they who would wed must be done with their mooning;
So let the churn rattle, see well to the cattle,
    And pile the wood by the barnyard gate!

Richard Watson Gilder

Overleaf
FALL COLOR
Tunbridge, Vermont
Bob Clemenz

The Fieldmouse

Where the acorn tumbles down,
    Where the ash tree sheds its berry,
With your fur so soft and brown,
    With your eye so round and merry,
Scarcely moving the long grass,
Fieldmouse, I can see you pass.

Little thing, in what dark den
    Lie you all the winter sleeping?
Till warm weather comes again,
    Then once more I see you peeping
Round about the tall tree roots,
Nibbling at their fallen fruits.

Fieldmouse, fieldmouse, do not go
    Where the farmer stacks his treasure,
Find the nut that falls below,
    Eat the acorn at your pleasure,
But you must not steal the grain
He has stacked with so much pain.

Make your hole where mosses spring,
    Underneath the tall oak's shadow,
Pretty, quiet, harmless thing,
    Play about the sunny meadow.
Keep away from corn and house,
None will harm you, little mouse.

Cecil Frances Alexander

To Autumn

Season of mists and mellow fruitfulness!
   Close bosom friend of the maturing sun;
Conspiring with him how to load and bless
   With fruit the vines that round the thatch-eaves run;
To bend with apples the moss'd cottage-trees,
   And fill all fruit with ripeness to the core;
      To swell the gourd, and plump the hazel shells
   With a sweet kernel; to set budding more,
And still more, later flowers for the bees,
Until they think warm days will never cease,
      For summer has o'erbrimmed their clammy cells.

Who hath not seen thee oft amid thy store?
   Sometimes whoever seeks abroad may find
Thee sitting careless on a granary floor,
   Thy hair soft-lifted by the winnowing wind;
Or on a half-reap'd furrow sound asleep,
   Drowsed with the fumes of poppies, while thy hook
      Spares the next swath and all its twined flowers;
And sometimes like a gleaner thou dost keep
   Steady thy laden head across a brook,
   Or by a cider-press, with patient look,
      Thou watchest the last oozings, hours by hours.

Where are the songs of spring? Ay, where are they?
   Think not of them, thou hast thy music too,
While barred clouds bloom the soft-dying day,
   And touch the stubble-plains with rosy hue;
Then in a wailful choir, the small gnats mourn
   Among the river sallows, borne aloft
      Or sinking as the light wind lives or dies;
And full-grown lambs loud bleat from hilly bourn;
   Hedge-crickets sing, and now with treble soft
   The redbreast whistles from a garden croft,
      And gathering swallows twitter in the skies.

John Keats

Photo opposite
ANTELOPE VALLEY
California
Alpha Photo Inc.

Old Fashioned Small-Town Park

From the first golden threads of the dawning
To the twinkle of firefly dark,
There's no place that's quite as lovely
As an old-fashioned small-town park.

A gazebo graces the center
'Mid a sea of China-blue flowers,
And you're lulled by the whisper of windsong
And the passing of soft summer showers.

Then the misty beams of the sunshine
Make latticed-gold the weathered old floor,
And a garland of ivy is twining
Close 'round the wide-arching door.

There's a spot where folks can play horseshoes
And swings where children can play;
There, a pathway goes winding;
Sundials mark shadowed hours away.

Oh, can't you hear the mockingbird singing,
The trilling of thrush and of lark?
Come, let's spend the day once again
In an old-fashioned small-town park.

Rose Emily Houston

Photo opposite
BANDSTAND
Weston, Vermont
Alpha Photo Inc.

The Bucket

How dear to this heart are the scenes of my childhood,
   When fond recollection presents them to view!
The orchard, the meadow, the deep-tangled wild-wood,
   And every loved spot which my infancy knew!
The wide-spreading pond, and the mill that stood by it,
   The bridge, and the rock where the cataract fell,
The cot of my father, the dairy-house nigh it,
   And e'en the rude bucket that hung in the well —
The old oaken bucket, the iron-bound bucket,
The moss-covered bucket which hung in the well.

That moss-covered vessel I hailed as a treasure,
   For often at noon, when returned from the field,
I found it the source of an exquisite pleasure,
   The purest and sweetest that nature can yield.
How ardent I seized it, with hands that were glowing,
   And quick to the white-pebbled bottom it fell;
Then soon, with the emblem of truth overflowing,
   And dripping with coolness, it rose from the well —
The old oaken bucket, the iron-bound bucket,
The moss-covered bucket arose from the well.

How sweet from the green mossy brim to receive it,
   As poised on the curb it inclined to my lips!
Not a full blushing goblet would tempt me to leave it,
   The brightest that beauty or revelry sips.
And now, far removed from the loved habitation,
   The tear of regret will intrusively swell,
As fancy reverts to my father's plantation,
   And sighs for the bucket that hangs in the well —
The old oaken bucket, the iron-bound bucket,
The moss-covered bucket that hangs in the well!

Samuel Woodworth

Overleaf
CALIFORNIA AT SOLVANG
Ed Cooper

Growing Up

by Russell Baker

Morrisonville was a poor place to prepare for a struggle with the twentieth century, but a delightful place to spend a childhood. It was summer days drenched with sunlight, fields yellow with buttercups, and barn lofts sweet with hay. Clusters of purple grapes dangled from backyard arbors, lavender wisteria blossoms perfumed the air from the great vine enclosing the end of my grandmother's porch, and wild roses covered the fences.

On a broiling afternoon when the men were away at work and all the women napped, I moved through majestic depths of silences, silences so immense I could hear the corn growing. Under these silences there was an orchestra of natural music playing notes no city child would ever hear. A certain cackle from the henhouse meant we had gained an egg. The creak of a porch swing told of a momentary breeze blowing across my grandmother's yard. Moving past Liz Virts's barn as quietly as an Indian, I could hear the swish of a horse's tail and knew the horseflies were out in strength. As I tiptoed along a mossy bank to surprise a frog, a faint splash told me the quarry had spotted me and slipped into the stream. Wandering among the sleeping houses, I learned that tin roofs crackle under the power of the sun, and when I tired and came back to my grandmother's house, I padded into her dark cool living room, lay flat on the floor, and listened to the hypnotic beat of her pendulum clock on the wall ticking the meaningless hours away.

I was enjoying the luxuries of a rustic nineteenth-century boyhood....

Editor's Note: Russell Baker began his career in journalism in 1947, when he was hired by the Baltimore Sun. *In 1954 he joined the* New York Times, *for which he covered the White House, Congress, and national politics. He has written his "Observer" column for the* Times *since 1962. In 1979 he won the George Polk Award for Commentary and the Pulitzer Prize for Distinguished Commentary. His columns were most recently collected in* So This Is Depravity. *He received the 1983 Pulitzer Prize for biography for* Growing Up. *We are pleased to reprint this excerpt about Baker's childhood years.*

Shootin' Marbles

Around a ring upon the ground
We used to see boys kneeling down —
Shootin' marbles.
With fingers clenched and knuckles raw
Each tightly gripped his trusty taw —
Shootin' marbles.
"Knuckles down," they would repeat
Whenever someone tried to cheat —
Shootin' marbles.
The game of life they still play fair
From lessons learned while playing there —
Shootin' marbles.
These lads have now become old men
Who often dream they're boys again —
Shootin' marbles.

W. C. Ferrell

The River, On

The river, on from mill to mill,
Flows past our childhood's garden still:
But, ah! we children never more
Shall watch it from the water-door!
Below the yew it still is there —
Our phantom voices haunt the air
As we were still at play,
And I can hear them call and say:
   "How far is it to Babylon?"

Ah, far enough, my dear,
Far, far enough from here —
Yet you have farther gone!
   "Can I get there by candlelight?"
So goes the old refrain.
I do not know — perchance you might —
But only children hear it right.
Ah! never to return again!
The eternal dawn beyond a doubt,
Shall break on hill and plain,
And put all stars and candles out,
Ere we be young again.

Robert Louis Stevenson

Keepsake Mill

Over the borders, a sin without pardon,
  Breaking the branches and crawling below,
Out through the breach in the wall of the garden,
  Down by the banks of the river, we go.

Here is the mill with the humming of thunder,
  Here is the weir with the wonder of foam,
Here is the sluice with the race running under —
  Marvellous places, though handy to home!

Sounds of the village grow stiller and stiller,
  Stiller the note of the birds on the hill;
Dusty and dim are the eyes of the miller,
  Deaf are his ears with the moil of the mill.

Years may go by, and the wheel in the river
  Wheel as it wheels for us, children, today,
Wheel and keep roaring and foaming for ever
  Long after all of the boys are away.

Home from the Indies and home from the ocean,
  Heroes and soldiers we all shall come home;
Still we shall find the old mill wheel in motion,
  Turning and churning that river to foam.

You with the bean that I gave when we quarrelled,
  I with your marble of Saturday last,
Honoured and old and all gaily apparelled,
  Here we shall meet and remember the past.

Robert Louis Stevenson

Train Time

Clickity clack, clickity clack,
A train is coming down the track!
Its rhythm hums along the rails,
Its engine whistle wails and wails

A lonely note the wind will tear
To scatter echoes everywhere.
Skippity hop, skippity hop,
We run to where the train will stop

For sacks of mail and people too.
There goes the switch, the train is due!
See, how the engine slithers past,
And right behind, but much less fast,

As though to capture every eye,
The silver cars go sliding by.
They slow down one by one until
Up front the giant wheels are still;

But in a minute now the train
Will hum along the tracks again,
To stop in towns I never see
And thrill small boys, who wait, like me.

Viney Wilder Endicott

Autumn

With what a glory comes and goes the year!
The buds of spring, those beautiful harbingers
Of sunny skies and cloudless times, enjoy
Life's newness, and earth's garniture spread out;
And when the silver habit of the clouds
Comes down upon the autumn sun, and with
A sober gladness the old year takes up
His bright inheritance of golden fruits,
A pomp and pageant fill the splendid scene.

There is a beautiful spirit breathing now
Its mellow richness on the clustered trees,
And, from a beaker full of richest dyes,
Pouring new glory on the autumn woods,
And dipping in warm light the pillared clouds.
Morn on the mountain, like a summer bird,
Lifts up her purple wing, and in the vales
The gentle wind, a sweet and passionate wooer,
Kisses the blushing leaf, and stirs up life
Within the solemn woods of ash deep-crimsoned,

And silver beech, and maple yellow-leafed,
Where Autumn, like a faint old man, sits down
By the wayside a-weary. Through the trees
The golden robin moves. The purple finch,
That on wild cherry and red cedar feeds,
A winter bird, comes with its plaintive whistle,
And pecks by the witch-hazel, whilst aloud
From cottage roofs the warbling bluebird sings,
And merrily, with oft-repeated stroke,
Sounds from the threshing floor the busy flail.

Oh, what a glory doth this world put on
For him who, with a fervent heart, goes forth
Under the bright and glorious sky, and looks
On duties well performed, and days well spent!
For him the wind, ay, and the yellow leaves,
Shall have a voice, and give him eloquent teachings.
He shall so hear the solemn hymn that Death
Has lifted up for all, that he shall go
To his long resting place without a tear.

Henry Wadsworth Longfellow

Thoreau's Woodpile

Every man looks at his wood-pile with a kind of affection. I loved to have mine before my window, and the more chips the better to remind me of my pleasing work. I had an old axe which nobody claimed, with which by spells in winter days, on the sunny side of the house, I played about the stumps which I had got out of my bean-field. As my driver prophesied when I was plowing, they warmed me twice — once while I was splitting them, and again when they were on the fire, so that no fuel could give out more heat. As for the axe, I was advised to get the village blacksmith to "jump" it; but I jumped him, and, putting a hickory helve from the woods into it, made it do. If it was dull, it was at least hung true.

Green hickory finely split makes the woodchopper's kindlings, when he has a camp in the woods. Once in a while I got a little of this. When the villagers were lighting their fires beyond the horizon, I too gave notice to the various wild inhabitants of Walden vale, by a smoky streamer from my chimney, that I was awake.

> Light-winged Smoke, Icarian bird,
> Melting thy pinions in thy upward flight,
> Lark without song, and messenger of dawn,
> Circling above the hamlets as thy nest;
> Or else, departing dream, and shadowy form
> Of midnight vision, gathering up thy skirts;
> By night star-veiling, and by day
> Darkening the light and blotting out the sun;
> Go thou my incense upward from this hearth,
> And ask the gods to pardon this clear flame.

Hard green wood just cut, though I used but little of that, answered my purpose better than any other. I sometimes left a good fire when I went to take a walk in a winter afternoon; and when I returned, three or four hours afterward, it would be still alive and glowing. My house was not empty though I was gone. It was as if I had left a cheerful housekeeper behind. It was I and Fire that lived there; and commonly my housekeeper proved trustworthy. One day, however, as I was splitting wood, I thought that I would just look in at the window and see if the house was not on fire; it was the only time I remember to have been particularly anxious on this score; so I looked and saw that a spark had caught my bed, and I went in and extinguished it when it had burned a place as big as my hand. But my house occupied so sunny and sheltered a position, and its roof was so low, that I could afford to let the fire go out in the middle of almost any winter day.

Henry David Thoreau

Photo opposite
WOODPILE
Fred Sieb

Readers' Reflections

'Neath the Hickory Nut Tree

'Neath the hickory nut tree
Stands a cottage so small
With vines clinging close
To the side of the wall.
It has not been painted
In many a year,
And yet it holds memories
So precious, so dear.

Once the grass in the yard
Sparkled bright in the dew,
And the flowers, when blooming,
Were glorious to view.
A little rose trellis
Stood close to the door,
And all summer long
There bloomed roses galore.

At the edge of the garden,
In a place set apart,
Leaned a weathered grape arbor
So dear to my heart.
The years, now long past,
Which were then, oh, so gay
Make me think of us children...
How we used to play.

Now and then as I sit
In the old rocking chair,
Rocking back through the years
To that favorite somewhere,
I know that no matter
How far one might roam,
There is nothing brings joy
Like the road that leads home.

Loise Pinkerton Fritz

Tomorrow's Harvest

Harvest fruits hang ripe and mellow,
Yellow gleams the goldenrod,
Tasseled thistledown is blowing,
Sowing next year's seeds abroad.

All my dreams, like migrant swallows,
Follow every dancing leaf,
And my heart holds autumn pleasure,
Treasure far beyond belief.

Alice Mackenzie Swaim

A Memory

Put it away to remember,
This beautiful thing that you feel,
Wrap it and tie it, then send it to you;
Make it a dream that's real.

Put it away in your heart, dear,
To relive a million times o'er.
Keep it forever a treasured thought;
Save it to cherish more.

Open it when you are lonely,
Keep it aglow with love,
Careful to always put it away,
Sacred as heaven above.

Put it away as a keepsake;
Then in the years to come,
This memory that you save today
Will last till a lifetime is done.

Garnett Ann Schultz

Harvest Blessings

Golden harvest time is here,
Our crops are gathered in;
The fruits and vegetables we raised
Now fill each crate and bin.

My shelves are stocked with fruit I've canned,
And in each jar I'll hold
The memory of a summer day
In winter's bitter cold.

Our children play with falling leaves
Beneath a peaceful sky,
While from my kitchen drifts the scent
Of homemade pumpkin pie.

I have just one request, O Lord,
That is, each day I start,
Please never once let me forget
To have a grateful heart.

Marian Constance Oaks

Editor's Note: Readers are invited to submit poetry, short anecdotes, and humorous reflections on life for possible publication in future *Ideals* issues. Writers will receive $10 for each published submission. Send material to "Readers' Reflections," P.O. Box 1101, Milwaukee, Wisconsin 53201.

Tapestry

This may we know, however small our work,
It is our own to do, and if we shirk,
Or if we pass it with averted head,
No other hands can do it in our stead.
We are possessors of a certain gift
Of sacrifice or service that may lift
Another's burden. This shall bring content,
Knowing that for this reason we were sent,
That by a simple word or gesture we
Might add some color to life's tapestry.
Our lives may be a flower, a climbing vine,
Or merely background for the vast design,
And if we weave in crimson or in gray,
For this brief interval that we can stay,
The beauty of the whole lies in the art
With which each unknown craftsman does his part.

Dorothy P. Albaugh

Photo opposite
PHLOX
Freelance Photographers Guild

Nature's Economics

I t's early autumn and in the Northeast a Grand Economy begins. September makes the announcement: Nature is back on the goldenrod standard.

Apparently it all has something to do with the fact that the silver dollars are ready, those paper-pearl coins minted right on little money trees.

A brisk commerce begins. The wind trades loosestrife seeds for the scent of ripe apples. A wisely miserly squirrel, investing heavily in dried currants and sunflower seeds, does his banking in a hollow log. Field mice, those most creative thieves, pilfer each other's savings and make safe deposit boxes of the boots you've left in the garage or the broken flower pots under the porch steps.

The underground crackles with consumer news: there's a good berry rummage down by the stone wall, woodpecker's having an acorn auction in the old oak, a pumpkin is growing not ten feet from the mole's north tunnel.

Chipmunk families go shopping in the flower garden, forming a self-service line at the anemone bulbs. Later, they may trade them back to you for hickory nuts, two for one.

Any morning now a thick, wet fog, like the pulp of clouds that have pressed too closely together, will coat the meadow. When the sun punches through, the silly spider will think she has trapped a treasure of diamonds in her web. She'll find herself bankrupt by ten o'clock.

Fair trade does not always prevail. For trees, the price of autumn's glory is discriminatory. Maples, soon to lose all their brilliant assets, pay mightily; the evergreens not at all.

The law, if you're self-supporting, is that it's best to be industrious now. Only the fat cows, discoursing on the bounty of their summer pastures, can afford to be idle. They stand and admire their wrap-around murals painted red and gold and russet, knowing that high-yield accounts have already been established for them in bulging barns and silos.

Experienced field managers know the value of good bargaining. A corporation of crows convenes on a telephone pole to argue group travel rates for wives and children. Winter stay-at-homes gather to balance the nut budget and scrutinize the seed monopoly of the greedy blue jay.

It's all very reasonable, really. When the world is so full, allocations need to be made so cycles can continue.

Even now Nature is negotiating a new contract with us: if we'll take a dreary, gray November, she'll trade us for a green and yellow May we won't believe.

Patricia Myruski

Fall Preserves

Cider Jelly

4½ cups sugar
4 cups apple cider
1 box (1¾ ounces) powdered fruit pectin

To make jelly, measure sugar and set aside. Measure cider into a large saucepan. Add fruit pectin; mix well. Place over high heat and stir until mixture comes to a hard boil. Immediately add all sugar. Bring to a full rolling boil and boil hard 1 minute, stirring constantly. Remove from heat and skim off foam with metal spoon. Ladle jelly boiling hot into jars to within ½ inch of the top. Wipe sealing edge. Seal with two-piece vacuum seal lids according to manufacturer's directions. Process 5 minutes in a boiling water bath canner. Yields 5¼ cups or about seven 6-ounce glasses.

Pear and Cranberry Jam

3 cups prepared fruit (about 2 pounds ripe Bartlett pears and 1 pound cranberries)
1 teaspoon grated orange rind
5 cups sugar
¾ cup water
1 box (1¾ ounces) powdered fruit pectin

Peel, core, and finely chop about 2 pounds ripe Bartlett pears. Measure 2 cups into large bowl. Grind about 1 pound cranberries. Measure 1 cup and add to pears. Stir in orange rind; add sugar. Mix well and let stand. Mix water and pectin in small saucepan; bring to a boil and boil 1 minute, stirring constantly. Stir into fruit mixture. Continue stirring about 3 minutes. (There will be a few remaining sugar crystals.) Ladle jam boiling hot into jars to within ½ inch of the top. Seal with two-piece vacuum seal lids according to manufacturer's directions. Process 5 minutes in a boiling water bath canner. Yields about 7 medium size glasses.

Plum Relish

2 pounds fully ripe plums
¼ to 1 teaspoon each cinnamon, cloves, allspice
½ cup vinegar
6½ cups sugar
½ bottle liquid fruit pectin

Pit plums; do not peel. Chop very fine, and measure 3½ cups into a very large saucepan. Add spices and vinegar. Thoroughly mix sugar into fruit in saucepan. Place over high heat, bring to a full rolling boil, and boil hard 1 minute, stirring constantly. Remove from heat and stir in fruit pectin immediately. Then stir and skim for 5 minutes to cool slightly and prevent floating fruit. Ladle relish boiling hot into jars to within ½ inch of the top. Seal with two-piece vacuum seal lids according to manufacturer's directions. Process 5 minutes in a boiling water bath canner. Yields about 8 cups or ten 6-ounce glasses.

Pumpkin Butter

3½ cups cooked pumpkin (one 29-ounce can)
1 tablespoon pumpkin pie spice
1 box (1¾ ounces) powdered fruit pectin
4½ cups sugar

To make the butter, measure 3½ cups pumpkin into a large saucepan. Add spice and fruit pectin to the pumpkin and mix well. Place over high heat and stir until mixture comes to a hard boil. Add all sugar immediately and stir. Bring to a full rolling boil and boil hard 1 minute, stirring constantly. Remove from heat. Ladle boiling hot into jars to within ½ inch of the top. Seal with two-piece vacuum seal lids according to manufacturer's directions. Process 5 minutes in a boiling water bath canner. Yields about 5½ cups or seven 6-ounce glasses.

Photo opposite
FALL BOUNTY
Gerald Koser

When the Frost Is on the Punkin

When the frost is on the punkin and the fodder's in the shock,
And you hear the kyouck and gobble of the struttin' turkey-cock,
And the clackin' of the guineys, and the cluckin' of the hens,
And the rooster's hallylooyer as he tiptoes on the fence;
O, it's then's the times a feller is a-feelin' at his best,
With the risin' sun to greet him from a night of peaceful rest,
As he leaves the house, bareheaded, and goes out to feed the stock,
When the frost is on the punkin and the fodder's in the shock.

They's something kindo' harty-like about the atmusfere
When the heat of summer's over and the coolin' fall is here —
Of course we miss the flowers, and the blossoms on the trees,
And the mumble of the hummin'-birds and buzzin' of the bees;
But the air's so appetizin'; and the landscape through the haze
Of a crisp and sunny morning of the airly autumn days
Is a pictur' that no painter has the colorin' to mock —
When the frost is on the punkin and the fodder's in the shock.

The husky, rusty russel of the tossels of the corn,
And the raspin' of the tangled leaves, as golden as the morn;
The stubble in the furries — kindo' lonesome-like, but still
A-preachin' sermuns to us of the barns they growed to fill;
The strawstack in the medder, and the reaper in the shed;
The hosses in theyr stalls below — the clover overhead! —
O, it sets my hart a-clickin' like the tickin' of a clock,
When the frost is on the punkin and the fodder's in the shock.

Then your apples all is gethered, and the ones a feller keeps
Is poured around the celler-floor in red and yeller heaps;
And your cider-makin's over, and your wimmern-folks is through
With their mince and apple-butter, and theyr souse and saussage, too!
I don't know how to tell it — but ef sich a thing could be
As the Angels wantin' boardin', and they'd call around on *me* —
I'd want to 'commodate 'em — all the whole-indurin' flock —
When the frost is on the punkin and the fodder's in the shock.

James Whitcomb Riley

HALLOWEEN PROMISE

Moon light —
Moon bright —
What will children
See tonight?

A big black witch
A fearsome cat
A goblin bold
A one-eyed bat
A ghost, an elf
A gypsy Queen
On this the eve
Of Halloween.

Moon light —
Moon bright —
What will children
Hear tonight?

A lone owl's hoot
Laments and squeaks
A cat's meow
A stair that creaks
Winds that cry
A latch that clicks
On Halloween
The eve of tricks.

Marguerite Gode

Photo opposite
HALLOWEEN
Fred Sieb

WHOO ?

"WHO — WHOO — WHOO
can it be?"
asks Blinky, the owl
in the sycamore tree.

"WHOO — are these pranksters
that troop into town
on Halloween Eve
when the dark settles down?

"WHOO — is the pirate
that leads the parade?
WHOO — is the elf
and the shy gypsy maid?

"WHOO — is the witch
in her high pointed hat
riding a broomstick
and leading her cat?

"WHOO — bobs for apples,
trades trick for treats?
WHOO — lights gay lanterns
along darkened streets?

"Where did they come from;
where will they go?
Poor little Blinky
is anxious to know."

Somebody tell him,
give him a clue
so he'll stop asking us,
"WHOO — WHOO — WHOO?"

Marguerite Gode

To Autumn

O autumn, laden with fruit, and stained
With the blood of the grape, pass not, but sit
Beneath my shady roof; there thou may'st rest,
And tune thy jolly voice to my fresh pipe;
And all the daughters of the year shall dance!
Sing now the lusty song of fruits and flowers.

''The narrow bud opens her beauties to
The sun, and love runs in her thrilling veins;
Blossoms hang round the brows of morning, and
Flourish down the bright cheek of modest eve,
Till clust'ring Summer breaks forth into singing,
And feather'd clouds strew flowers round her head.

''The spirits of the air live on the smells
Of fruit; and joy, with pinions light, roves round
The gardens, or sits singing in the trees.''
Thus sang the jolly Autumn as he sat;
Then rose, girded himself, and o'er the bleak
Hills fled from our sight; but left his golden load.

William Blake

Butternut Harvest

Gladys Taber

Now is the time to go out to the woods for butternuts and hickory nuts and hazelnuts. The upper pastures are grey-green and tranquil, the deciduous trees flame against a sky as soft as the breasts of a dove. The old greystone ledges are warm, the light is golden on the fallen burrs. The butternuts are dark and sticky, the hickory nuts have a green plastic case and underneath are smooth as ivory. The hazelnuts are fringed with cinnamon on the outer case and have an exquisite tri-cornered shape.

George's cows stand in pleasant aimlessness in the driftway as we go by. A big buck rabbit goes lippety lippety into the thicket. A wandering country cat pauses to eye us soberly, then sleeks away on her own serious business.

We carry old gunnysacks and we fill them, it is impossible to stop when the treasure is there for the gathering. Midway we sit on a big rock that is frosted over with lichen and eat our ham and cheese sandwiches and drink the hot coffee from the thermos. Even as we eat, nuts plop down, surely bigger and better than any we have yet gathered! The squirrels have been at work too, many of the nuts are only shells by now.

Staggering under the weight of the sacks, we finally come home, feeling we have done a very worthwhile thing. Never mind that we never do get all the nuts shelled. We crack some with a flatiron on the hearthstone, but we never really get to them all. I surmise it is more fun to adventure in the autumn woods than to dig out the tiny meats afterward with a pick.

Cracking and shelling butternuts takes real devotion. I get as far as one butternut cake — what could be more delicious — and then I decide to wait. The nuts can season. As for the hickory nuts, it would take a freight-car load to make a decent amount of meats. Hazelnuts shell easier, and are possibly more rewarding.

We used to have black walnuts too, but the black walnut tree was a victim of an early hurricane and is just a memory now.

After all, I think, as I sweep up the shells and nurse my bruised thumb and measure a half cupful of nutmeats, it is the joy of the gathering that is important, rather than the end product!

From STILLMEADOW DAYBOOK, copyright 1955 by Gladys Taber. Copyright renewed 1983 by Constance Taber Colby.

Overleaf
ASTER FILIGREE
H. Armstrong Roberts

After Apple-Picking

My long two-pointed ladder's sticking through a tree
Toward heaven still,
And there's a barrel that I didn't fill
Beside it, and there may be two or three
Apples I didn't pick upon some bough.
But I am done with apple-picking now.
Essence of winter sleep is on the night,
The scent of apples: I am drowsing off.
I cannot rub the strangeness from my sight
I got from looking through a pane of glass
I skimmed this morning from the drinking trough
And held against the world of hoary grass.
It melted, and I let it fall and break.
But I was well
Upon my way to sleep before it fell,
And I could tell
What form my dreaming was about to take.
Magnified apples appear and disappear,
Stem end and blossom end,
And every fleck of russet showing clear.
My instep arch not only keeps the ache,

It keeps the pressure of a ladder-round.
I feel the ladder sway as the boughs bend.
And I keep hearing from the cellar bin
The rumbling sound
Of load on load of apples coming in.
For I have had too much
Of apple-picking: I am overtired
Of the great harvest I myself desired.
There were ten thousand thousand fruit to touch,
Cherish in hand, lift down, and not let fall.
For all
That struck the earth,
No matter if not bruised or spiked with stubble,
Went surely to the cider-apple heap
As of no worth.
One can see what will trouble
This sleep of mine, whatever sleep it is.
Were he not gone,
The woodchuck could say whether it's like his
Long sleep, as I describe its coming on,
Or just some human sleep.

Robert Frost

HOBBY HORSE

Jump on your horse
And I'll take mine —
We'll ride for hours today!
The sun is warm;
The weather fine —
Come, come! Giddap! Away!

Away down hills!
Up mountains tall!
We'll race without a care!
O'er bridges high,
Through tunnels dark —
We'll visit everywhere!

We'll trot to town
For lollipops
And rainbow ribbons gay!
We'll gallop on
To Uncle Bart's
And draw a load of hay!

We'll canter right
Through Jungle Town!
We'll make those tigers run!
We'll ride out to
The circus lot —
The clowns will be such fun!

We'll stop to see
The Crooked House;
We'll find the cookie tree!
I'll tie my horse
And you tie yours —
We'll picnic — you and me!

Come, come, let's go!
We're off! Goodbye!
Be home tonight, of course —
But what a ride
A child can have
Upon his hobby horse!

Marion Tubbs

Photo opposite
HOBBY HORSE
H. Armstrong Roberts

Long Ago

I once knew all the birds that came
   And nested in our orchard trees;
For every flower I had a name —
   My friends were woodchucks, toads, and bees;
I knew where thrived in yonder glen
   What plants would soothe a stone-bruised toe —
Oh, I was very learned then;
   But that was long ago!

I knew the spot upon the hill
   Where checkerberries could be found,
I knew the rushes near the mill
   Where pickerel lay that weighed a pound!
I knew the wood — the very tree
   Where lived the poaching, saucy crow,
And all the woods and crows knew me —
   But that was very long ago.

And pining for the joys of youth,
   I tread the old familiar spot
Only to learn this solemn truth:
   I have forgotten, am forgot.
Yet here's this youngster at my knee
   Knows all the things I used to know;
To think I once was wise as he —
   But that was very long ago.

I know it's folly to complain
   Of whatsoever the Fates decree;
Yet were not wishes all in vain,
   I tell you what my wish would be:
I'd wish to be a boy again,
   Back with the friends I used to know;
For I was, oh! so happy then —
   But that was very long ago!

              Eugene Field

The Child in the Garden

When to the garden of untroubled thought
I came of late, and saw the open door,
And wished again to enter, and explore
The sweet, wild ways with stainless bloom inwrought,
And bowers of innocence with beauty fraught,
It seemed some purer voice must speak before
I dared to tread that garden loved of yore,
That Eden lost unknown and found unsought.
Then just within the gate I saw a child —
A stranger-child, yet to my heart most dear —
Who held his hands to me and softly smiled
With eyes that knew no shade of sin or fear;
"Come in," he said, "and play awhile with me;
I am the little child you used to be."

Henry van Dyke

Henry van Dyke, "The Child in the Garden" from THE POEMS OF HENRY VAN DYKE.
Copyright © 1920 by Charles Scribner's Sons. Reprinted with the permission of Charles
Scribner's Sons.

Merry Autumn Days

We hail the merry Autumn days
  When leaves are turning red;
Because they're far more beautiful
  Than anyone has said;
We hail the merry harvest time,
  The gayest of the year;
The time of rich and bounteous crops,
  Rejoicing and good cheer.

Charles Dickens

Autumn Fires

In the other gardens
   And all up the vale,
From the autumn bonfires
   See the smoke trail!

Pleasant summer over
   And all the summer flowers,
The red fire blazes,
   The gray smoke towers.

Sing a song of seasons!
   Something bright in all!
Flowers in the summer,
   Fires in the fall!

Robert Louis Stevenson

from Evangeline

This is the forest primeval.
  The murmuring pines and the hemlocks,
Bearded with moss, and in garments green,
  indistinct in the twilight,
Stand like Druids of eld,
  with voices sad and prophetic,
Stand like harpers hoar,
  with beards that rest on their bosoms.
Loud from its rocky caverns,
  the deep-voiced neighboring ocean
Speaks and in accents disconsolate
  answers the wail of the forest.

This is the forest primeval;
  but where are the hearts that beneath it
Leaped like the roe, when he hears in the woodland
  the voice of the huntsman?
Where is the thatch-roofed village,
  the home of Acadian farmers —
Men whose lives glided on
  like rivers that water the woodlands,
Darkened by shadows of earth,
  but reflecting an image of heaven?
Waste are those pleasant farms,
  and the farmers forever departed!
Scattered like dust and leaves,
  when the mighty blasts of October
Seize them, and whirl them aloft,
  and sprinkle them far o'er the ocean.
Naught but tradition remains
  of the beautiful village of Grand-Pré.

Henry Wadsworth Longfellow

Ernest Jack Sharpe

Ernest Jack Sharpe was born Ernest Sharpsteen in Wyoming Township, Kent County, Michigan, on July 8, 1888. He was the youngest of ten children.

His career was unusual and varied. When still a boy, he joined a circus, and for the next seven years worked in circuses and vaudeville comedy. Mr. Sharpe later joined a traveling theater company in which he worked as actor, playwright, and director.

His home on the lakeshore in Newago County, Michigan, occupied more and more of his time. In 1931 he gave up show business to open a lakeside resort. At about this time he began to write verse and adopted the pen name of Ernest Jack Sharpe.

Mr. Sharpe spent the rest of his life at his home on the lake. Because he was a great believer in the value of libraries, he made a down payment on the future home of the city library in White Cloud, Michigan. He later willed his entire estate to the library.

The Old Wooden Pump

In the back yard, in those dear days of yore,
Stood an old, wooden pump near the kitchen
    rear door.
'Twas all made of wood, from handle to spout,
And it squeaked to high heaven when you
    pumped water out.

It moaned and it groaned as the bucket would fill,
Then changed its tune to a screech loud and shrill.
No matter the season, it seemed to complain
With squeals, grunts and groans, as though 'twere
    in pain.

Sounds seemed unpleasant in those days of yore,
But now, how I wish I could hear them once
    more.
The song of that pump, now coming to me,
Would sound to my ears like a real symphony.

Memory Lane

I've a wonderful place in Memory Lane, a place
  that is wondrous fair:
A sparkling stream, a swimming hole. Once again,
  as a child, I am there
With grocery twine, a willow pole. My hook is an
  old bent pin,
And I spit on the worm, to bring good luck, before
  I toss it in.

The fish I catch don't amount to much, as grown-
  up fishing goes,
But to me they're the very best fish on earth, as my
  childish boasting shows.
And I carry them proudly, as in the past, for all
  the world to see
And feel again that thrill of old come stealing
  over me.

'Tis a wonderful scene and it brings me joy as I
  live it once again,
Traveling a path through Childhood Land down
  dear old Memory Lane.

Those Good Old Days

How did we spend our evenings in those days of
  long ago,
Before we had the movies, TV, or radio?
Oh, maybe some neighbors would drop in for a
  little stay.
We'd have a round of pedro, or maybe checkers
  play.
Or we'd gather 'round the organ and sing a song
  or two,
Pop some corn, make taffy, or maybe fudge
  would do.

We'd have a jug of cider brought up from the
  cellar,
Also a plate of apples, rosy red and "meller."
Somebody then would crack some nuts and when
  we were well fed
And started getting sleepy, we'd meander off
  to bed.
Nothing much exciting, but to put it to the test
By comparing it with things today, somehow I
  liked it best.

Boyhood Memory

In memory I wander back in the past. I'm a
  barefoot boy again,
Going for cows 'long an old, rail fence, down a
  winding country lane.
It is evening and from over the hills there comes a
  bobwhite's cry,
While swallows sail on homeward flight across
  an azure sky.

My faithful, old dog is by my side, but every now
  and then
He sniffs in a corner of the fence to tell where a
  rabbit's been.
The warm sand oozes between my toes and I kick
  it into the breeze
Where little clouds of dust are formed and wafted
  through the trees.

I whistle a tune as I stroll along, as happy as I
  can be,
For not a worry or trouble or care is there to
  bother me.
It is only a memory from out the past, but I wish
  I could live it again,
Going for cows 'long an old, rail fence down a
  winding country lane.

Overleaf
SAND DUNES STATE PARK
Utah
Ed Cooper

Something Told
the Wild Geese

Something told the wild geese
    It was time to go.
Though the fields lay golden
    Something whispered, "Snow."
Leaves were green and stirring,
    Berries, luster-glossed,
But beneath warm feathers
    Something cautioned, "Frost."

Reprinted with permission of Macmillan Publishing Company from BRANCHES GREEN
by Rachel Field. Copyright 1934 by Macmillan Publishing Co., Inc., renewed 1962 by
Arthur S. Pederson.

All the sagging orchards
   Steamed with amber spice,
But each wild breast stiffened
   At remembered ice.
Something told the wild geese
   It was time to fly,
Summer sun was on their wings,
   Winter in their cry.

Rachel Field

Evening

Alone on the bench at the foot of the palm,
At that loveliest of hours, the Sunday night calm,
There's a faint hint of dew as the night shadows fall
And a drowsy accent to the night bird's last call.
The sun drifts away to its home in the west,
On the pink and gold pillows to take a rest.
When the sky turns to gray and the pinks and blues blend,
It's the loveliest hour to think of a friend.

Annie Fitzpatrick

Sky Prayers

Sea sunsets, give us keepsakes.
Prairie gloamings, pay us for prayers.
Mountain clouds on bronze skies —
    Give us great memories.
Let us have summer roses.
Let us have tawny harvest haze in pumpkin time.
Let us have springtime faces to toil for and play for.
Let us have the fun of booming winds on long waters.
Give us dreamy blue twilights — of winter evenings — to wrap us in a
    coat of dreaminess.
Moonlight, come down — shine down, moonlight — meet every bird
    cry and every song calling to a hard old earth, a sweet young earth.

Carl Sandburg

Photo opposite
BIKES AT SUNSET
H. Armstrong Roberts

The Wild Swans at Coole

The trees are in their autumn beauty,
The woodland paths are dry,
Under the October twilight the water
Mirrors a still sky;
Upon the brimming water among the stones
Are nine and fifty swans.

The nineteenth Autumn has come upon me
Since I first made my count;
I saw, before I had well finished,
All suddenly mount
And scatter wheeling in great broken rings
Upon their clamorous wings.

I have looked upon those brilliant creatures,
And now my heart is sore.
All's changed since I, hearing at twilight,
The first time on this shore,
The bell-beat of their wings above my head,
Trod with a lighter tread.

Unwearied still, lover by lover,
They paddle in the cold,
Companionable streams or climb the air;
Their hearts have not grown old;
Passion or conquest, wander where they will,
Attend upon them still.

But now they drift on the still water
Mysterious, beautiful;
Among what rushes will they build,
By what lake's edge or pool
Delight men's eyes when I awake some day
To find they have flown away?

William Butler Yeats

Overleaf
MIST AT SUNSET
Fred Sieb

October Butterflies

Grieve not, my friend, when winter winds appear
To bend the oak and sing their mournful song,
When the colored leaves of autumn bid farewell;
For airborne leaves are just October butterflies
That dance and settle on the frosty earth,
To make a sun-hued patchwork quilt
And warm the seeds for springtime's birth!

Emily Scarlett

Haze Gold

Sun, you may send your haze gold
Filling the fall afternoon
With a flimmer of many gold feathers.
Leaves, you may linger in the fall sunset
Like late lingering butterflies before frost.
Treetops, you may sift the sunset cross-lights
Spreading a loose checkerwork of gold and shadow.
Winter comes soon — shall we save this, lay it by,
Keep all we can of these haze gold yellows?

Carl Sandburg

From GOOD MORNING, AMERICA, copyright 1928, 1956 by Carl Sandburg. Reprinted
by permission of Harcourt Brace Jovanovich, Inc.

It's Our 40th Birthday! IDEALS 1944-1984

Our next anniversary issue features a tribute to the season of bounty and a historic look at the first Thanksgiving.

We celebrate this land of plenty in our Thanksgiving Ideals issue with classic poetry and prose and breathtaking color photography.

But we don't want to sing our own praises. Satisfied readers have shared these comments with us: "Just a short note to say how very, very much I enjoy Ideals. It clings to the old-fashioned ideal of home and family, togetherness as a people, as a nation. We need this so much at a time when things seem to be falling apart.... Please keep up the same format and never try to go modern" (M. P., McAllen, Texas). "I just have to comment on this fabulous book; it is beautiful and inspiring.... The breathtaking artistry is a joy to behold" (D. L., Minneapolis, Minnesota).

Share an Ideals gift subscription with family and friends, beginning with our Thanksgiving Ideals. Surround your loved ones with beauty and inspiration year round.

ACKNOWLEDGMENTS

TAPESTRY from BY QUILL AND CANDLELIGHT by Dorothy P. Albaugh; TRAIN TIME from A SALUTE TO AMERICA by Viney Wilder Endicott; EVENING from A LITTLE BIT OF HEAVEN by Annie Mayhew Fitzpatrick; A SONG OF EARLY AUTUMN from THE COMPLETE POEMS OF RICHARD WATSON GILDER; recipes for CIDER JELLY, PEAR AND CRANBERRY JAM, PLUM RELISH, and PUMPKIN BUTTER by Darlene Kronschnabel from COUNTRY SCENE, Vol. 1, No. 2, copyright 1976 by Ideals Publishing Corporation; WHEN THE FROST IS ON THE PUNKIN from THE BEST LOVED POEMS OF JAMES WHITCOMB RILEY; the poems by ERNEST JACK SHARPE are from his book MEMORIES OF YESTERYEARS. Our sincere thanks to the following people whose addresses we were unable to locate: Marian Constance Oaks for HARVEST BLESSINGS and Marion C. Stacy for HALLOWEEN PROMISE and WHOO by Marguerite Gode.